www.finishinglinepress.com

It Started with
the Wild Horses

poems by

Ingrid Keriotis

Finishing Line Press
Georgetown, Kentucky

It Started with
the Wild Horses

ACKNOWLEDGMENTS

The following poems have appeared in these literary magazines, newspapers, books, and websites:

"Exception," "Koropi, Greece," and "Traveling from Home": *4More: A Benefit Journal*
"Thea": *American River Review*
"September": *Blue Unicorn*
"Bedside": *Currents*, a publication of *the Union*
"Wild Horses": *Flumes*
"Up Late Reading Wendell Berry," "Sculpting," "Extinguished," and "Mytilene":
    Inscape
"Uncivilized," "Light on Skin," "Songs," and "May for Zoe": *More than Soil, More than Sky: The Modesto Poets*, Quercus Review Press
"Dishes": *Poetry Now Online*
"Waters": *Quercus Review*
"Jobs," "The Poet of Trader Joe's," "Guests": *Sisyphus*
"Fragile," "Naptime": *Stanislaus Connections*
"somewhere i have never travelled": *Steam Ticket*
"Monday": *Talking River*

Publisher: Leah Maines
Editor: Christen Kincaid
Cover Art: Anastasia Keriotis
Author Photo: Kathleen Truax
Cover Design: Leah Huete

Printed in the USA on acid-free paper.
Order online: www.finishinglinepress.com
                    also available on amazon.com

Author inquiries and mail orders:
Finishing Line Press
P. O. Box 1626
Georgetown, Kentucky 40324
U. S. A.

Table of Contents

Thanks

Bio

This book is for Zoe and Eleni

"Is the past a story we are persuaded to believe in, in the teeth of the life we live in the present?"

—Wright Morris

Guests

Sometimes I imagine a whole family
living in my master bedroom.

They've been driven out of the camp in Calais
or found their way here
from a muddy site in Macedonia.

They're overjoyed with the faucets,
and wood that used to be my bookshelf
now feeds an open fire
where women sit, stirring stew, chatting
as they once did in their own kitchens.

On my bed small children are curled up, asleep
and at my desk in the corner,
older children turn my worn jeans
into makeshift shoes.

In spite of the new visitors, my family
still sleeps in beds, walks clean floors,
eats in a well-stocked kitchen
until we are all satisfied.

I peer into my master bathroom
just in time to see a boy
who looks older than his eight years
perched on the counter in front of the mirror,
lips in a gap-toothed smile.

His hands are at work
on a loose tooth,
one he will nestle in the heart
of his palm, shaken, torn
having survived a journey
halfway around the world.

Philadelphia, 1973

Backing up on all that green
almost all the way
to the left field fence,
he thought of Nebraska.

The threshers, the combine, the tractor
auctioned off when he was ten.

It had started with a ball in his crib.
Playing catch for him was daily bread.
At church his father copied stats
on the bulletin and passed it over
with a quiet hand.

Nebraska,
even the name tasted like honey.

Wide skies and shifting clouds
the earth wearing its fields of cut grain
like a big shorn animal,
low dark fields lying below a sky
in early spring, waiting.

His fingers clasp the stitching of the ball
but he's gone out to his father's field
to get soil under his fingernails
so he can carry in his body
something of home.

The Orchard

"You went from parched to overflow in the blink of an eye."
—Anne Lamott

Like wood catching fire
on a bed of smoke,
almond blossoms suddenly appear
and I think, foolishly,
that I can capture the moment.

This is what stuns me most
as I stand at the roadside:
each year I think
it will be different.

I might be able to hold that sight
full in my chest,
the sun and breeze, too, even the wild impulse
to climb on top of my car
for the best view
and my mad dash across a two-lane highway
with my camera.

Rising up from green valley and grey trunk
the precise blur of thousands of white petals
pulses in me
the full catastrophe of spring.

somewhere i have never travelled

For Dimitri, with apologies to e.e. cummings for stealing

Somewhere I have never traveled—
into your dreams.

Who am I there? Do I show up
at your high school,
in your kindergarten class?
Am I the girl sitting next to you
with the bouncy curls
who smiles when you look away
and peeks at you through her fingers
at nap time?

Or maybe it is Sunday and
you're driving us in a derby.
Bracing ourselves in a Model T
we go around turns
and laugh like we're praying.

Perhaps I am a movie star me,
sipping red wine,
standing taller than you in heels
while we spin dancing
around the room, luminous.

Really, I would be happy if I could be
even a moth in the corner
sitting there, hoping
you don't jerk in your sleep
or wake suddenly, anxious.

I would wish I could become again
a sleeping self
you might lay a quiet arm across.

You could whisper to me
one of your stories.
Even if, in the morning
I won't remember
any of the words.

Dishes

Dear Mike,
Here's the thing about the dishes:
I wouldn't let my mom get rid of them,
so I took them home.

When you moved in, I was angry.
You came from Oregon and took my mom
out dancing late,
then moved into our house
with your orange cat and several floor mats.
Later you threw out all we'd saved
in our fabulous drawer of junk.

You brought these blue-rimmed dishes
we ate from every night: pesto, stir fry,
foods I'd never had.
You cooked and the house rang
with laughter.

I want to thank you now, for the dishes.

Especially the bowls
with their creamy white centers.
It is amazing the heft
of an oval ceramic dinner plate,
how many times
it can be passed hand to hand
on its way somewhere.

Your hands don't touch anything anymore:
not the smoothness of a round edge,
or the silence of a soup spoon,
not the bounty of a shallow blue-rimmed dish
filled with all it can hold.

Thea

The gnarled olive branches
of Thea's hands showed how her knuckles
kneaded bread, that her fingers knew
on their own how to wash and sew.

Her body, once young and shining
in a swimsuit on the sand
became infirm, bent.

We often see the house only for its broken
windows, its yellowed weeds in pots
that once held bright red geraniums.

If someday she exists again
outside the body's fragile frame,
she may scatter as mist
or lay herself down as water
to stroke the land as waves do,
unified and separate,
like the child who flies
in dreams, her fingers full of rain.

Fifteen

In a dark black box theatre,
breath wild, I watched.

The graceful man drew leotard-clad women
to him and touched lightly
curves of torsos
as feminine arms rose like feathers.

He held them as they arched and swayed
and my one life wish,
penned in a spiral-bound notebook was gone.

In my wooden theatre seat
I wished instead
for hands like those
to stop their erotic chase and pursue
in a room or in a car or on a beach
with cliffs above and stars, my flesh.

Nighttime

In the dim light I could see
the sheets drawn around
my mother's face.

I crept into her room, knowing
I wouldn't be able to stay.
She was lost in the sleep of working mothers,
the world of dreams
I dared to drag her from.

Standing so close I could've touched
the lines of her nighttime face,
I called to her like an incantation.

Her eyes opened, ones that showed
the balance of irritation and compassion
I knew so well.
She would send me back
into my bedroom of fears.
But, no.

This time,
she opened the blankets around her
for a moment
and I—nearly shaking with surprise—
nestled beside her warm body,
the one whose every flaw
filled me with joy.

Anatomy of Grief

In memory of Nick Anast

You were no longer in your boat,
water dashing over its slim sides.
The bay was a purple wave of gain and loss.

You were peaceful, your friend said,
as you treaded water on the wide moon
of ocean.

I remember your deliberate walk,
your garden Buddhas
and dug-up wild game bones,
the spun-glass smile you gave the world.

You came to me while I slept,
asking me to carry bundles of shirts
calm on their hangers.

I'm not ready for you to go, I said.
You said, *It had to be in water.*

This is the hardest thing to learn:
drifting from your ruined kayak
that day into a rough ocean
was both how and when
you had to leave us.

Once your body
no longer shivered, it rocked
so deep in earthly waters
it could not be found

below the filtered daylight
into the filament of seaweed
that twined into your soft and billowing hair.

Umbrella

This has been bothering me for years:
how I left an umbrella in her office.

Her name was Crow
and in her class I wrote about redwoods.
One student wrote about the religion
of lawn care in Central Michigan.

And then there was Chuck
who wrote papers his instructors
wished they'd written,
who stopped smiling at me in class
after I cut my long blond hair.

One night I was bold
and took the open mic
in a drafty college house
to read about scarves
that danced down the back
of a rich woman's neck.
Marianne, who loved Chuck still,
sang to compete with my poem.

And all this time my instructor's office
held my umbrella, the one
with the wooden handle
I left during a mandatory office visit,
the one my father gave me
for life in the Northwest.

Maybe, when I didn't come for it, she used it
on a rainy walk to the bus stop.

I couldn't go back up those stairs,
sit in that chair next to all those books.
Though it sat in a corner, waiting for me
I didn't dare go claim it as mine.

Sculpting

For my grandmother

My little brother fell
from the second-story window
while Mom was in the basement,
sculpting.

At the hospital,
his head was stitched up,
his breaks were set straight.

At home Mom gathered up
all of her projects:
a head with the beginnings
of a face, a bust with no finality of form,
so many figures, nearly finished.

I left my homework behind
to go and see what she had done,
but they were already gone.

I stared at those empty shelves
where not even
a clay-encrusted tool remained,
knowing what those shapes could have become,
her finger sliding along
their fragile bones.

Monday

Out my car window, I saw you leap
in open-toed shoes over puddles,
a bag on your shoulder with its heavy load.
Unlike me, you didn't check the weather
before leaving for class.

Perhaps you were too busy
finding a new roommate, a new
look, a textbook
you should've bought last week.

Maybe you just told your parents
you're moving out, broke,
now in love with girls.

Maybe you're mad at your
therapist and tired from all that
crying into Kleenexes
while you discuss
your anger over your dad's
neglect, drinking, insults.

I see you with your dyed hair
and face of subtle discontent
from where I now stand
in front of the room.
I am ironed and ready
with my white board pens
lined stiffly in their trays.

While you watch the eyes of
the man-boy two rows over,
questions burn
inside your pierced and silent skin,
and I stack my notes
under the glow of the projector.

You will never know
in this moment before my lecture begins
how much I envy you.

Jobs

In America, to work to help others
is often to be poor:

changing diapers on other people's babies,
washing dishes we leave behind
in the restaurant tub,
helping others' grandparents down
the long hallway that leads to the bathroom.

The janitor puts on his uniform at 3 a.m.
so quietly while others in his household sleep,
his back bent from sweeping, mopping,
his hands curled as he reaches for his trousers.

Imagine instead a reversal: these workers on vacation
somewhere with gentle sun and smooth sand.
They fling themselves into silken waves,
eat pineapples and papayas
sculpted to look like fans,
sleep underneath billowing
clouds of comfort.

And the rich man must perform for his lunch
like the unwashed child on the metro
whose hands maneuver so swiftly
along the curves and keys
of his accordion.

May for Zoe

I wait to breathe in
the buckeyes by the river again
as I did in the early days
before bed rest,
when I would tell you about spring

how in California it comes
early, like the contractions
three months premature,
your home pushing in on you,
the pressure of each wave.

You will emerge
into a world of daisies and pollution,
walnut orchards and unending highways,
muddy rivers, uncharted caves.

I will stare at the lines
in my own long fingers
and recall the forgotten home
I left inside my mother—
the now quiet place for me
she carries with her still.

Traveling from Home

One night I took strange vows
and licked the spilled wine from the tile floor
the way I once saw a priest do.

Another night, I clung
onto my mother's house by only a beam
while a tornado blew toasters
and knives past my horizontal body.

I need to tell you that once
you and I had an arrangement on the side.
I had at least two other loves,
and you had yours.

In one dream, the flat, prickly
backyard of my childhood home grew
past the madrones and bays
into a world I'd never seen
with hills the color of cantaloupes
and I was like the woman
in the Maxfield Parish, standing on the cliff
in ecstasy, arms reaching
for the startling moon.

But always in the morning I am thirty-nine again,
still convinced of these exquisite lies,
with circles like shores under my eyes
and hair that's been caught in
the messy wind of my pillow.

Puppies

Although her friend said
they should never tell, she did.

The station was calm and quiet
and the policeman nice, but firm,
persistent in asking her to say
words she did not want to use
to describe what she wished
she'd never seen.

They drove grey streets.
In each figure, each man's face
she looked for him.

She and her friend had held
the new puppies in their arms,
brought them over to his truck to see.
In the Safeway parking lot
they backed away,
hurried to return the puppies to the box
on a friend's porch.

That night the darkness of the hallway
crept into her dreams,
the sight of the man,
his hand pointing to the penis
coiled in his naked lap,
his lips in an absurd grin.

And she remembered the puppies.
New, small, and wriggling,
they had tumbled over their mother
once back in the box,
so sure of what was good in the world,
and where it could be found.

Another Part

She is another part
of my own body, human warmth
like skin in rays of the sun.

Her head tucked into my arm,
the milky smell of her is in my clothes.
Dipping my nose deeply into her soft hair,
I can say for sure, *this one is mine.*

I remember a darkened room
of sweat and sighs, sheets in disarray,
our limbs wrapped around each other
like winding smoke.

Before her smell was upon me,
it was yours.

The Loch

I stood beside the small,
nameless loch in Scotland
on my failed honeymoon
for my failed marriage.

Its lapping was quiet but sturdy,
the wind stirred the water just enough,
rocks loomed above me like sentries.

This loch, of course, does not need me
to remember it, but I think of it now:
moist hills surrounding
that grey-blue water as they did
twenty years ago when I knew
I was standing
in a green ring of fire.

Naptime

The only naptime sound
is my chopping of garlic
as careful blade meets board.

Outside, paper thin petals
in the bee-swabbed almond
pop from buds
and torn branches are strewn
from the wild storm
that brought my daughter
three weeks ago.

So silent now as she sleeps
like feathers at rest,
the hands of the monk in his robed lap,
blossoms papering the mud,
white dots with translucent veins.

My seasoned hands' rhythm
is all that breaks the silence
that holds her gently like a vase.

Even dictators, soldiers
without tenderness began
so pure in their newborn sleep,
eyelids resting like doves.

Faults

I don't iron your slacks
or make your lunch,
sliding it to rest in the silvery
insides of your lunchbox. I don't
clean receipts out of your car
or tell you every day
you're wonderful.

I don't lovingly pack
your overnight bag, folding
the crisp white origami of undershirts.
I don't clear your plate
from the table, chicken bones
lined up like driftwood.

There are times I don't even
let you
finish
your sentence.

But each day your metronome heart
confers life from its calm cage,
I still plan
to build a small home for myself
in that place between your
right shoulder and your chest
where it's smooth and the days are quiet.
There I will nestle on that most tender part
of your unbroken world.

California, Fall 2017

In the photo, the orange glow
lazing over the hillsides is beautiful
until you realize it is spilling flames
down into a neighborhood.

Houses are full of familiar messes:
the stack of sea glass
in an old pot, well-worn
books in a corner,
a daughter's boots by the door, waiting
for someone to clap mud
from their soles.

And what about the things in that one kitchen drawer:
half a notepad, a bottle of dried glue, twisty ties—
will these all burn, too?

Fire will arrive hungry, make embers
of the things you loved, the things you ignored,
the things you will release right before
you know they're gone.

Fragile

Standing in the kitchen
roses on our table, petals
pooling beneath their vase,
you tell me
now you appreciate rosebushes.

We never should have let
the ones outside the window die,
the ones planted
by the old woman.

Beside you, elbows on the table,
I am thinking of yesterday
how in Virginia the professor barred
the gunman at the door
while his students escaped
out the windows.

I once heard the words,
"The softest thing in the universe
overcomes the hardest."
I was not ready to hear this then
but now I know your hands,
the skin of my daughter's face,
how each life settles like fallen water.

What would we call life
if it didn't end, would we even
call it by a name
if it was always ours?

Asking

For a student

His eyes said,
Don't ask me anything, just give
me the goddamn assignment.

Don't tell me a story about Vietnam
that's just a story to you.
Don't read me a war poem
if you've never felt the blood
as you got your field cross tattoo.

And don't ask about my buddy.
I'm at this college and he isn't so fuck
your comma splices and gelled hair,
screw the projector and buttons you hit
with a polished nail,
your water bottle and the water in it
that slides down your safe and protected throat.

And don't look at me
like there's so much you want to ask,
like you're so sure I want to tell.

Unitarian Church, Marin, 1978

Even as a child, I knew our church
was a place people escaped to instead of from.
There was the man who wore
printed dresses and carried a purse,
the lesbian couple in Birkenstocks,
too many Jews to count,

my mother, the agnostic,
and my father, the minister.

He was always under pressure
to get religion right
for those so scared
to let it into the room.

I searched for God
in the diamond eyes we made
of string and sticks,
in the Seders we celebrated,
singing "this little light of mine."

In the dark, we passed flames hand to hand,
a square of white paper catching
hot drips of wax from our candles,
and our prayers were sent out,
I'm still not sure to whom.

Waters

Today is as clear as polished stone
and here I sit in a still-wet chair,
trying to feel delighted.

It is too quiet.
The fierce creek is now only
a murmur and no wild rain beats on my house.

Gone, too, is the deep blue light
that sprang at five o'clock
through the trees,

driving me from my house
into wildness, mist
in the folds of snowy hills.

Where have the waters gone,
the rivers going madly somewhere,
brown and free and driven?

I am the only one here
thinking about yesterday.

The saturated fields and oaks
feeling the sun on their backs
have gone on to other things.

Songs

Soft as splinters pulled from blankets
offered like sweaty pennies
from an opened palm,
their screeching, annoying tunes
are like church music from a bad organ
and a half-vacant choir
when the priest,
holding the holy book in his hands,
gives less light than the winter sun
streaming through stained glass.

I haven't said anything.
I have no time to say it,
no space to fill
like freshly-washed wine glasses
or stockings ready to hold
the shape of gently curved toes.

The din of children's voices creeps
over my ears like mites.
Repetitive, thin little songs
keep me from mine.

Exception

virga: wisps of precipitation evaporating before reaching the ground

Because no moment ever lasts,
I store loss like a box on a high shelf:

the day I stood in that long,
yellow California grass
and saw a path that went
only one way, from him,

the night I lay on the couch,
my body unable to hold
a life that grew within.

Once, I cradled a college boy's
head of sun-dusted hair in my lap
as we traveled down a bumpy road
into the wilderness.

And I thought *this might be the exception,*
that time might pause or
even stop.

That time and self, the road and him
might like virga in the desert
for a brief while,
suspend.

Thessaloniki

The scents of cigarette smoke
and jasmine drift past
as I watch people.
Heads bob on bodies' long stalks,
as they glide along the shore of sidewalk.

Shop owners and tourists,
deer in the traffic of the grass,
stop, chew, gaze, and scatter.

Always searching, this crowd of colorful fish
swims in a cloud that passes
beneath buildings framing blue sky
and ruins like the impenetrable trunks of trees
remind us of the sand and ash
in store and street.

Love, 1960

He was a chaos of possibility:
each self a little fire, he was
a boy with a mother gone.

Living with his grandmother,
he wasn't allowed to dance,
to drink, to think of himself as a body.
She taught him
to fill his mug with absence,
to ignore his longing, familiar as breath.

He didn't love himself
but loved the other boys,
their sandy cheeks, how they bumped
into one another laughing on the school bus.
He would look away, not knowing
what words to use to lie.

His friends saw her first. She was
hard to catch, pretty
in her flower print dress, hair rolled
smooth, smile promising something.

How could she know about the others' bodies
he wanted to press against
in a hallway around a corner
of the high school.

In his arms he held her
but no truth was allowed in,
until it came in the form of a lover
with a body and a life like his,
a wife, children.

AIDS took his secret away
but when he sat alone
in silence, she knew.

Lies melted like soil in the rain
and the love that was almost real
was washed away.

4 a.m.

I hold hair back from her face
as she leans over a bucket
she clutches with tired hands.

I notice her slim neck and face gaunt,
clothes piled up on the floor
of a once-clean room, her sister,
sleeping in childish comfort
a few feet away.

Things may get worse before
they get worse: the number
of pill bottles on the counter,
the slips of paper in my purse
with doctors' numbers and pharmacists' notes,
the feeling of wanting to be someone else.

I have looked at others
passing on the sidewalk
or standing in line in front of me
as they place snacks on a grocery belt
or absentmindedly scratch
the back of an ankle with the toe of a shoe.

Wiping up the floor or mixing
powdery medicine with juice,
I have seen myself living another life:
pulling a boy's Superman shirt over
his healthy body as he
flings his arms in the air,
brushing a quietly waiting horse,
as I listen to the soft foghorn
of its breathing.

I could be driving down a road
with so much sky above me
it would be like an ocean.

I would even sit in a cubicle
somewhere crunching numbers
or reading repetitive pages of text—

I would do anything rather
than sit with my daughter,
the one with a turned-up nose
and a singing voice like bells,
as she shakes with the force
of trying to empty an already empty stomach.

Looking into her eyes
dull with the aches of her body,
love presses against the inside of my skin,
and I shudder to think that I would trade.

Clothesline

Afternoon heat ripples
through the olive trees
and the smell of summer grass
like baking bread
rises in the warmth of the afternoon.

A breeze shifts through the cotton dresses,
dripping on the line.
Socks and shirts held taut by their shoulders
wait for hands to pull them apart again.

They will be plucked from where they hang
once sun-ripened
so torsos and limbs
can slide themselves in and be held.

Pathways

If we could keep
what was *then*
and what is *now* apart,
how fresh each day would be

but we are wet pages,
covered with blurred lines of ink.

When you yelled, it was like a branding.

Callouses have grown
on my seasoned feet,
I am full of the trails
we climbed, clung to, and released.

I may wash off yesterday,
slough off the 30,000 cells of me,
take the antidote
for your particular poison,
but in the morning, am I clean?

Wild Horses

It started with the wild horses.

Had I really seen them that day
from my '91 Civic,
as they galloped untamed
through the sagebrush,
a blue storm rising as their backdrop?

Did my body lay down
in a hot spring filled with stars
in the middle of the desert?

Had I ridden a river at dawn
between brown canyon walls,
dug deeply with my oars
under the shallow river's skin,
seen the sun spread out before me
on wet stones?

If the stories you tell
become like dreams,
then images behind your eyes
can't know,
if, in their hues of blue and grey, brown and gold,
they even remember you.

Stirring Peanut Butter, 6:00 a.m.

Moms in commercials
don't slop the oily part of the peanut butter
onto the side of the jar.

With wet hands and a baby on a hip,
my eyes gaze across a crumb-laden counter
at my toddler, stealing sips
from my mug of strong black tea.

"I deal in fluids," I tell a friend,
a way to explain where I've been:
breast milk, teething slobber, toddler's pee
on the Mexican rug.

A plastic, whirring, breast-cupping pump,
the only road to free time.
I ask my mother, "What was new motherhood
before breast pumps?"
"We gave you formula when we went out
and we didn't worry."

Now we know about colostrum
in mother's milk, lead in toys,
chemicals in bottles, mercury in vaccines—

"Mommy mommy mommy mommy"
a song throughout the day
just a word but a change—
from a being
to a being, needed.

I am thankful for grandmothers,
flowers plucked
from the mouths of bees
by small hands,
snacks in shining packaging

And an endless well
of something deeper than love
that ebbs but is replenished.
Spilling over, it gives itself away.

Never Left

One evening, he paced their neighborhood
of square lawns and one-story homes
with a gun in his hand,
looking for perpetrators
when his young wife hadn't gotten off the expected bus.

His wife could not imagine
what he had done at nineteen
while she was in college
drinking beer from plastic cups
and writing essays into slim blue notebooks.

She read novels to try to understand.
Once, she read a paragraph aloud to him
about a soldier whose friend died beside him
in the muck and mud on a day of no glory,
and he ran, sick, to the toilet,
to kneel on the cold stones of the linoleum.

In the bathroom, men in green fatigues
stood in worn boots:
ghosts to her, men to him.

Uncivilized

Because I have a garden
I might become uncivilized:
mud might walk in on my boots,
spiders and moths
might enter through my open door.

And if they don't, I have no reminder
of the wildness we've undone
for armchairs and DVDs.

I long to plant, dig, scatter seed,
but there are days of mail, piles of clothes—
domestic clutter
ensnares me.

I am like those before me
who carried extra gunpowder
in fear of bears
but at least they slept outside like evening grass,
kissed with dirt on their lips.

My fingernails too clean,
I am alarmed by my lack of scent,
embarrassed by soft feet
unprepared as they are
for whatever lies ahead.

Winter Night

When the night is an indictment
that you are not like the others
so lost in dreams they dance in their beds

and dawn is a distant reality
as it spreads itself
across the shore of another continent,
you remember the world is a place
where a man can stand on top of his car
with another man's organs in his hand
and declare this is a victory

where the person we all want to inspire us,
to lift us up with his lofty words
takes us instead to the gutter
to play in garbage.

But as the night deepens,
you see something else:

At times, you drive as if no one else
is on the road, but you and your life.
Once, you hit your child
just to let the anger out,
another time you slammed your words
into a lover's ear
with force like a physical blow.

Your own complicity comes
as dawn does, slowly—
arriving to stretch itself
across the tips of your eyelashes.

September

The idea of September:
children's lives, unopened,
on the playground.

That child stomping leaves—
at 57, he will lie,
holding in his arms, his wife,
a hairless bird.

The little girl laughing
on the swinging bars
and the boy with the sad face, like a puppet—
in 40 years they will see each other
wandering the aisles of the supermarket,
looking for canned soup, razors,
their faces mirrors flashing
with recognition.

Leaves scratch their sun-burned bodies
along the street with rasping voices,
then come to rest in dry, discarded curls—
I want them to be like children,
flying away.

Athens Subway, 2013

They must've been working together:
the woman across from me
saying something in a foreign tongue
and the woman beside me,
hands hidden in a long skirt.

Suddenly, she tries to open
the zippered section of my bag.
I startle and pull away,
swing my overfull bag in front of me,
clutch what is mine.

The women exit quickly.
No one's attention strays
from themselves, their sweaty hands,
gripped tightly to subway poles.

Inside my bag, I feel for my camera
loaded with its images of Greece:
the Parthenon in its ruined whiteness,
fishing boats, their paint peeling into the sea,
and the graffiti at the park
behind the broken swings,
spray-painted words saying,
"All is lost."

Bedside

For my father

She combs her hair a little
with one hand, I take her other arm
and guide it around me.

I am seven, and she has polio.

She recites poems
that saved her when in the iron lung,
when every breath was a struggle.
"There is a pleasure in the pathless woods.
There is a rapture in the lonely shore . . ."

I listen, not knowing all the words,
run her comb through my short hair.
I stare at its tortoise shell handle,
as she slips into sleep.
Dark curls lie on her pillow,
eyelashes quiet as night.

She wakes, calls to my father,
"Come get Steven. Go out and play ball."
Why is she calling him to take me away?
He doesn't come.

So she'll let me stay,
I am as still as her silent legs
beneath the sheets.
I try to memorize her face,
even its grimaces as she shifts her shoulders.
I hold on to the feeling
of that arm around me in its soft pink sleeve,
so heavy it is almost holding me.

"Do you love me?" I ask, as
I have asked before.

She says my name quietly.
I hug her middle, stiff like a doll's.

As a man I will remember
how I had to ask, that I wasn't sure.

Light on Skin

For a student

What if you could string together
the best parts of years, days, weeks?
I would leave out the ones I lost
when I didn't know the president,
the season, the backyard outside
my dusty window.

The four o'clock sun hits
rows of walnut trees, while the drumbeats
of machines tearing out a distant orchard
descend on the earth.

No chemicals in the air today,
the birds are taking deep breaths.
Hungry cows face me
in the austere light.

Past an abandoned barn I turn
for home, the brown winter grass
brushing my legs.
I would never know I was ten minutes
from the city, those old apartments
like dirty shoes, the alleys
of broken glass, syringes.

I would never know if I hadn't
reminded myself just now,
wind in my fingers:
without addiction, I wake to life.

Extinguished

Breath leaves my body. My bones
loose, I am dancing
wandering the streets,
no longer in need of sleep or dreams.

I am lifted by wings
like those of Garcia Marquez' old man,
transported above the furry
backs of hills and dusky
clouds of oaks.

No body contains me, no mind
with its hundreds of lists
to trail me like receipts in the wind.

I have forgotten
how I used to walk around the house,
when each movement was a task.

I am flames without a grate,
the self, having just slipped out
of its sleeve.

School Counseling Session, 1987

A poem in two voices

I

She sits before me in black cords
and misshapen jacket,
the hand-me-downs of divorce.
Her brown bangs provide
a shelf for hiding.
I ask and ask and she offers more,
tipsy with the truth.

I hope she won't
need to come back. I can help
the cutters, the twelve-year-old
who replaces his mother's
vodka with water,
the girl who pulls hair from
her head, a palace of white lumps.

"Each day will be better," I tell her.
"It's hard for your mom, too."
I write my notes, wishing everyone
could be as eloquent as she is
in her displeasure.

II

I sit in the cold school
chair, surrounded by inspirational
posters of cats in soft light.
Opening the door of foggy glass,
she looks down, invites me
into a cave of bright light
soaring through dusty blinds.

Talking is like taking

a pill too large for my throat,
chalky but nutritious.
I force it down.

My science teacher
with the grey shaggy hair
brought me here. He noticed
my life's medieval torture—
stretched as I was
fingertips to fingertips, crown to soles.

It rolls out of me:
how I speed up putting my key in the lock
at dad's, rush into his house
to make sure he hasn't left for good,
how I go from one parent's house to another
with a backpack, like someone selling
things door to door.

Her eyes blink at me
and I wonder, does she sleep,
does she dream, does she cry?

Mom said once only crazy girls
considered suicide.

"It will get easier," the counselor says.
"Don't be so hard on your mother."
My mother, the instigator,
who choose difficult
like it's a brand of shoes.

I have gotten used to such lips
that move up and down the street like taxis,
each word gone
without a goodbye.

I peel a cuticle down
to the red, work a strip
of skin back and forth.

I can't even see the mouth of the whale
as it swallows me whole.

Koropi, Greece

Mice holes dot doorways
and dust clings to bedsheets
in this tin-roofed house where
Efterpi died two summers ago.

Our choice of vacation home
is unexpected, I think,
as I wring out our clothes.
They drip onto the concrete
and veins in my arms stand like raised maps.

In the garden, the old *feta* tins spill over
with flowers and plants.
Our girls, one and three, splash
in a metal basin warmed by sun,
wash salt water from their skin.

We are a mile from the Aegean
where jellyfish spin
like curtains in the current
and across from a bakery,
where in the afternoon we find *kolouri,*
a hot ring of sesame bread
we hold in our hands.

The Albanian woman behind
the counter doesn't smile,
but when our three-year-old gives her coins,
she adds a cookie to
the bag with the bread.

She probably wonders why Americans
are staying at the dead woman's house,
why we always look like
we've come from the beach.

My husband asks

how long she's lived in Greece.
She tells us she walked here in 1980.
Walked? he says, making sure he understands.

She and her husband needed to know
if—like Hoxha said—
the outside world was starving, too.
They made it over the mountains
to Greece, feet nearly blue
and cried when they saw
peoples' fat cheeks, his words proven untrue.

They live in a house like ours,
run at night even in a downpour
to an outdoor toilet,
twist beans from stalks in a garden,
walk to the songs of chickens and goats
telling the hour.

But soon, unlike our neighbors, we will leave,
a turquoise sea receding
below our sandaled feet.

Office Hour

"Would you rather be perceived
as passionate or intelligent?"
my professor asked me,
his face leaning down close to mine.

At nineteen, I hadn't expected
to have to choose.

His arm reached over the desk
to hand me back my writing,
so I could make revisions.

But twenty four years have passed
and I've changed my mind.

I don't want to revise away the self
or edit sentences down to their sterile centers.

Others will try to cram us
into their own tight spaces
just as we're coaxing out
the selves we no longer want to hide.

The Poet of Trader Joe's

She's singing out in front
of the Roseville Trader Joe's,
hair uncombed,
eyes drops of black moon.

I pause
in front of the chrysanthemums.
Automatic doors open and close
as people file inside.

I turn to her,
the window of her voice opens,
and the parking lot is left behind.

Her song is the hum of insects in the grass,
water so low in the well its life is an echo.

It is laborers in a green field,
hot sun stinging their backs,
singing
so no one will have breath left to cry.

Juicy

Consider the perfect sweetness
of a beet
as you tear your vegetables
limb from limb.

As you long to fill your emptiness
with their green promises,
notice the white bone of the romaine.
Open the cucumber, let the skin
slide across your knife.

Scatter insides to reveal
delicate cores and sticky seeds,
make a mess you'll be in no rush to clean.

Beet blood does stain
the longer you leave it to spill,
but take comfort: soon
you will not be as hungry
as you have been.

Playground Mouths

I didn't like him.
He was loud, brash
had big white teeth,
but I followed him
after the last bell rang.

It wasn't really a park,
just a triangle of weeds with two trees
behind a stretch of one-story houses
with little windows.

You've French kissed before, right?
he said, air filled with bees.
I said *yeah*, the lie coming easily.
He scooted towards me,
moving in.

His tongue flapped
like an errant flag.
I forced a smile, wiped my soggy chin.

It was repulsive, wet
but I knew it was supposed
to feel nice.
I shifted a little, hands
supporting me so the moist grass
wouldn't soak through
my favorite pants, the ones with pink hearts
sewn onto the back pockets.

The Workshop

They sit at the feast, knives
at the ready, tablecloths spread,
plates about to receive.

They start with your tongue, cut
it out and dive in piece by piece.

It's chewy, but they enjoy it still.
Then they go in: legs, arms, torso—
they snarl over every section of you.

They save your eyes for last,
knowing they're a delicacy.
They disagree with what those eyes
have seen, loved.
They want to swallow your vision, to seize.

First the green is gone, then
the veins, eyelids, lashes.
Exacting fingers remove
until they have taken away
even the darkness that was yours
when you closed your eyes.

It was yours alone,
but somehow in their hunger,
they managed to take that too.

Empathy

Can the wildness in all of us
that sometimes shouts or scorns
show itself instead
in ecstatic love

for rain-washed leaves, great grey
mountains on the horizon,
every child's gaze?

When we grasp each other
in a night-time fervor, we feel it, too,
and when we surrender our bodies,
let them drop slowly
into dream.

Asleep, I travel roads I'll never see,
search for oil-streaked birds
by once-turquoise waters, crouch with mothers
in the darkness beneath the mahogany trees
of another continent.

Close your eyes.
Be in another's body for a moment,
feel their blood circle through intricate veins.
Now imagine it spill and fall.
Look, it blooms red, just like yours.

Spring

My sorrow is big
and ripe like an orange.
I twist at the roots.

Grief winds inside me,
air in my blood that hurts.
When the winding is done,
I open.

But the words reach you, fists
holding nothing. There are
no fresh, young leaves.

Spring comes over and over,
new, and we are never prepared.

River, Then

You are all those places she spent time
rivers, canyons, woods, tents
amid the smell of cool rivers and dried leaves.
Idaho, Washington, Redding,
where she stepped off the Greyhound
inhaling her California: rural, wild.

She chose her college
for the forest, plunged into the Pacific,
pushed apart water the color of light.

She floated rivers trying to make
a job of reading water
in places that made her want to land,
stop driving. But each time she did leave,
no idea where she would be in the end.

Now those places pull at you
grabbing your clothes like beggars.

You are someone else now
who lives behind a fence,
wears shiny shoes,
consults a calendar each day.

You wish to smell her scent
of sunscreen and warm rocks, but you can't
because every new day, she's left you again.

Dad's Place, 1992

Dad's house: two bedrooms
his with simple nightstand,
Pope books, baseball cards,
mine where I used to run in place
pounding the floor
when I couldn't sleep.

Kitchen: food mostly from Whole Earth,
healthy except for the chocolate,
an old dial phone, no microwave.

Cupboards: Swedish tins for pressing cookies,
plates and cups from Goodwill,
saggy vases from ceramics class,
beautiful bowls made by the gay potter
who lives down the road,
two banana bread pans—remember to dry
before putting away—
three knives, not very sharp.
Fridge: mostly condiments.

Living room: ugly over-stuffed chair
where a silly boy once sat
in disbelief when I told him
we weren't in love.

Weeknights: Dad asleep in the chair, glasses still on.
Saturday night: gone at his girlfriend's,
my lithe boy runner and I snuggled up
with Don Henley in our ears
and more on our minds.
Hearts: fresh washed linen
ready for use.

Remedial

He wrote about what it felt like when her fist
hit the skin of his face.
The girl beside him described
how her stepfather
had pushed in spite of her resistance
and one young man told how his mother
called him every bad name he had ever heard
and some that were new.

These people were supposed to have been
parents, parenting.

I had expected to teach the topic sentence, the use
of a transitional phrase,
how to write an essay so smooth
it could move logically
to a natural end.

But when I left for home
I could not bear to carry my bag beside me
so instead I hugged it close, desperate
to keep their stories out of the rain.

Mytilene

In California, my daughter
sings at the piano
"All day, all night Maryann
down by the seashore sifting sand."

All day all night the refugees
arrive. Greek children look up
from sand buckets, eyes shift from play
and Syrian children get out of rafts
with shaking legs.

Then the widows arrive,
walking down to the beach
in black dresses and sturdy shoes.

They hold and rock the toddlers
who've come from the sea,
smile for those who will post
their pictures for the world.

We watch, devices in our hands
and my daughter sings,
"All the little children love Maryann"

as all the little children
cross oceans of sand.

The Kiss

Behind his father's warehouse,
we would put our hands
over our mouths, lean our faces close
and pretend to kiss.

From soap operas I learned how:
twist head side to side slowly,
breathe deeply, hum.

In a run, with wet leaves underfoot
and in the air,
we slipped away into the redwoods.

One afternoon, we paused
to rest in a hollowed trunk
and hands left our lips—
I am not sure if mine was first, or his
to reveal what was soft and moist beneath.

I rushed home
aware of dusk in the trees.
I knew my mother would be there
stirring a hot pan while just underneath
a flame began its dance
on low heat.

Iris

In memory of Iris Chang, 1968-2004

The young journalist wanted to break
a six-decade silence,
to put what she'd learned into print.

Forgetting to sleep or eat, she wrote
the first book on Nanking's rape,
the Chinese people's torment,
wartime, 1937.

Even the Nazis were shocked
by the torture, the 300,000 dead.

She had sat in survivor's homes,
read diaries, looked at photos of live burials,
bodies nailed to walls.

She had let her body
fill with the stones of their stories.

The newspaper said she was haunted by those
it was too late to save with her listening.

Iris,
on that November morning,
you visited the hunting shop
to make your purchase,
drove Highway 17
headed into hills of black oak.

At the side of a dusty road,
you stopped, shed yourself
like a snake
and took the only way you saw
to escape being inside your skin.

Up Late Reading Wendell Berry

I can't sleep. Why not start being alive
right now at 12:30 a.m.
here with Berry's wood drake
and wild things, his day-blind stars
and still water?

And I am up late with
all the nights I've kissed you
all the grassy hills I've wandered,
days of soaking rain
coming from an open palm of sky,
the utter allure of an egret
hunting in the marsh
at the side of a busy highway.

And how about this?
That the sun hasn't disappeared for good
that a page of words feels
like a lover with a soft mouth

that a book can open everything
when just a moment ago
you were alone
in all the world.

Thanks

Many thanks to the Women's Writing Salon, Nevada County Arts Council, Pat Miller, Gail Entrekin, Judie Rae, Rebecca Tolin, Rachel Howard, Travis Davis and the writing group members, Suzanne Roberts, Rob Davidson, Kirsten Casey, and all of my Nevada County writing friends. Gratitude also to my community college students who remind me time and time again what perseverance means.

A thank you to Gillian Wegener, Gordon Preston, Sam Pierstorff, and all of the other Modesto poets, and to Dipali Murti and Karen Davies for their support and critiques. A huge thank you to Christopher Bakken and the wonderful Writing Workshops in Greece faculty, Molly Fisk and her Poetry Boot Camp, and my mentor, Lillian Vallee, who inspires not just with her writing but also with her spirit.

I am also grateful to my creative mother and sisters for their insights, and to my father who has been reciting poems to me since I was old enough to listen. A huge thank you to Jordan Rosenfeld, whose amazing book *A Writer's Guide to Persistence* should be on all writers' shelves, and to my talented sister-in-law, Anastasia Keriotis, for the cover photograph. And, of course, thank you to my husband, Dimitri, for everything.

Ingrid Keriotis is published in the anthology *More Than Soil, More Than Sky* and her poetry has recently appeared in *Sisyphus, Poetry Now, Steam Ticket, Flumes,* and *Blue Unicorn.* Since receiving her MFA from Eastern Washington University, she has taught English to community college students, who provide inspiration for many of her poems. Ingrid lives with her husband and two daughters in the Sierra Nevada foothills, where she spends her free time swimming in the Yuba River and walking under the pines.

CPSIA information can be obtained
at www.ICGtesting.com
Printed in the USA
FSHW020133151019
63005FS

9 781635 348934